This book belongs to:

Jennifer Ashley Clark
May 6, 1994

MESSAGE TO PARENTS

This book is perfect for parents and children to read aloud together. First read the story to your child. When you read the story a second time, run your finger under each line, stopping at each picture for your child to "read." Help your child to figure out the picture. If your child makes a mistake, be encouraging as you say the right word. Point out the pictures and words that are printed in the margin of each page. Soon your child will recognize the picture symbols and be "reading" aloud with you.

Copyright © 1992 Checkerboard Press, Inc., 30 Vesey Street, New York, New York 10007. All rights reserved.
READ ALONG WITH ME books are a registered trademark of Checkerboard Press, Inc., and are conceived by Deborah Shine.

ISBN: 1-56288-224-4   Library of Congress Catalog Card Number: 91-77733
Printed in the U.S.A.   0 9 8 7 6 5 4 3

The Story of Joseph

A Read Along With Me® Book

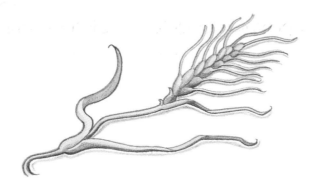

Retold by **Laurence Schorsch**
Illustrated by **Thomas Sperling**

Checkerboard Press
New York

Jacob

Joseph

Long ago in the land of Canaan lived

a man named . He had twelve sons.

Of all his sons, loved best.

day made a beautiful of many colors. When 's saw the of many colors, they were jealous. They hated and spoke to him only in anger.

 night had a dream. He told his about it. "We were all binding wheat sheaves in a field. My sheaf stood upright, and all of your sheaves bowed down to mine."

The became angry and asked , "Do you think that someday you will rule over all of us?" And they hated him even more.

Joseph

brothers

sheep

goats

Jacob

A while later 's were away tending their flocks of and . called and said, "Go. See if your are well and bring me word."

So traveled to where his were. But when the saw coming, they felt hatred for him. They said, "Let us kill ." But Reuben, the oldest of the , said, "We must not kill . Rather, let us throw him into some deep hole." For Reuben planned to return secretly to save . All the agreed. So they threw into a deep hole nearby.

Later that day some merchants were

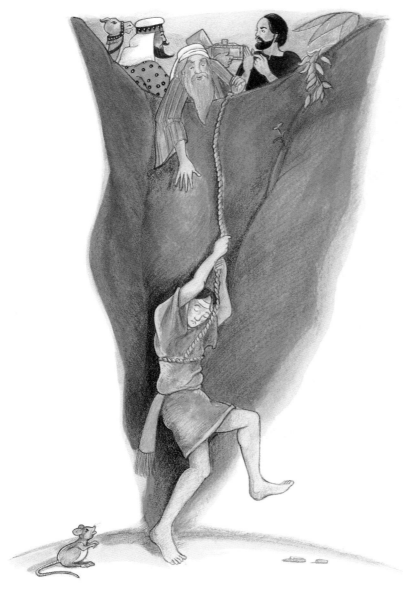

passing by on their camels. The said,

"Let us sell to those merchants." And

the took out of the hole and

sold him into slavery.

The  then dipped 's of many colors into the blood of a

They took the home to and said, "We found this of many colors, but we do not know if it belongs to ."

knew the at once. And

he wept and could not be comforted

because he loved so much.

The merchants took to Egypt

and sold him to a soldier. And all the while

God protected . Although he was a

slave in a strange country, soon

became known as a wise man.

It happened day that the

of Egypt had a dream that troubled him.

None of the wise men in the 's court

could tell him the meaning of his dream.

 of the 's servants told him of

's wisdom, and the sent for him.

one

pharaoh

pharaoh

Joseph

seven

cows

river

people

grain

The  told , "I dreamed that 7 fat cows came out of a river. Then 7 thin cows came out of the same river. And the 7 thin cows ate the 7 fat cows."

God revealed the meaning of the dream to . said to the , "The 7 fat cows are 7 years of plenty. The 7 thin cows are 7 years of famine. God is telling you that there will be 7 years of good harvest. But this will be followed by 7 years of famine. Your people must save grain during the 7 good years so that they will have grain for the bad years that will follow."

And the said, "I choose you,

, to watch over Egypt and to be the

keeper of the . You will be the most

powerful man in Egypt after me."

pharaoh

seven

people

grain

Jacob

Benjamin

As the 's dream foretold, there

were years of plenty. All the

stored . When the famine came,

there was  for all the in Egypt.

The famine was also in Canaan, and

 said to his sons, "Go to Egypt. Buy

 so that we may live." But would

not let , his youngest son, go to Egypt

for fear that some harm might befall him.

The other went to Egypt. When they came before to ask for grain, they did not recognize him. knew his at once, but he did not let them know who he was. The bowed down to , as their sheaves had bowed to his sheaf in 's dream so long ago.

brothers

Joseph

spoke roughly to his . "You

are spies!" he accused them.

The were afraid. "No, we are

honest men from Canaan. We are twelve

Joseph

brothers

is dead, and our

youngest is home with our father."

"If it is true that you have 1 more

 at home, you must prove it to me.

one

brother

grain

one

brother

brothers

pharaoh

"I will sell you , but of you must stay in Egypt. He will be kept prisoner until you bring your youngest to me."

So of the was put into the 's prison, and the other took the and returned to Canaan.

When the got home, they told

 what had happened and what they

had promised to do. But feared for

his youngest son, and he would not let

 go.

However, it was not long before all the

 that the had bought in Egypt

was eaten. The said to , "We

must have . We must go back to

Egypt and take with us."

The promised that they

would bring back home again.

Finally allowed to go. He

prayed to God to keep his sons safe.

Jacob

Benjamin

brothers

Joseph

Jacob

goats

sheep

When the came before again, they were very afraid. But said to them, "Do not fear. I am . Your hatred for me was evil, but God turned it to good. Many lives have been saved since I came to Egypt." And so and his were joyfully reunited and made a great feast.

Then said to his , "Go to Canaan and bring our father, , all our family, and your and . And we will live together in the land of Egypt."

So and all his family came to live in Egypt. When greeted his father, they fell into each other's arms and wept

tears of happiness.

And  and and all their family

lived together in the land of Egypt for

many years after.

Books I have read:

☐ David and Goliath

☐ Noah's Ark

☐ The Story of Jonah

☐ The Story of Joseph

The **Read Along With Me**® series is a collection of stories from the Bible, classic fairy tales and fables, and modern stories for parents and children to enjoy together.